A Walk Through the Dark Valley of Death

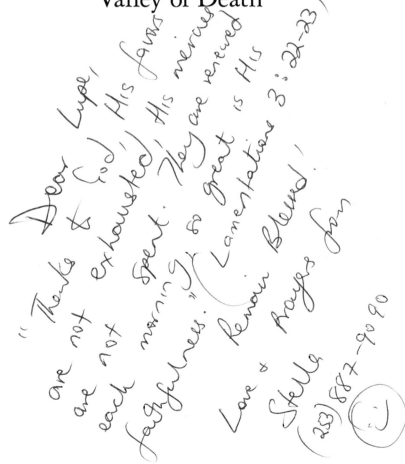

Dear Lupe,

"Thanks to God,) His favors are not exhausted; His mercies are not spent. They are renewed each morning; so great is His faithfulness." (Lamentations 3:22-23)

Remain Blessed!

Love & Prayers from

Stella
(253) 887-9090 :)

To order additional copies, please contact us.
BookSurge, LLC
www.booksurge.com
1-866-308-6235
orders@booksurge.com

STELLA
IHUOMA NNANABU

A WALK THROUGH THE DARK VALLEY OF DEATH

A PERSONAL STORY EXPRESSING
CONFIDENCE THAT GOD WILL HELP EVEN
IN THE WORST OF CIRCUMSTANCES,
INCLUDING THE DARK VALLEY OF DEATH.

2005

A Walk Through the Dark Valley of Death

TABLE OF CONTENTS

ACKNOWLEDGEMENTS

My soul magnifies the Lord and my Spirit rejoices in God my savior, for he has looked with favor on the lowliness of his servant." (Luke 1:46-48 a). On the human and practical side of things, my greatest appreciation and love go to my wonderful husband Jerry, for his infinite patience with me as a sick person, and during my recovery. Without his belief in me, his love and prayers, this book would not have been possible to write. He performed all the computer duties and edited my manuscript. He took time off from work to do all the cooking, groceries, the errands, the laundry, the bills and spent some time with me while I was home recuperating. I love you, honey. Thank you!

I owe a tremendous debt of gratitude to my three beautiful children - Somutoo, Chubie and Ihuoma for holding down the fort at home for the ten days I was sick in the hospital, and Daddy was gone all the time. You three are the "salt", the flavor in my life. Somutoo, thank you for being a good "temporary" dad and mom to your siblings, for all the dropping off and picking up from school, library, ballet, basketball practices and games. You are indeed a very loving, caring and responsible son and brother.

I am indeed indebted to my mom, dad, brothers, sisters, brothers in law, sisters in law, cousins, aunties and uncles. Mommy, Daddy, Lilian, Cas, Julia, Annie, Emeka, Ify, Uchenna, Nneka, Josy, Oby, Cletus, Clarice, Patrick, Augustine and Anna, thank you for all your fervent prayers, masses, novenas, visits, phone calls, cards, meals, flowers, jokes, tears and laughter. You made my difficult experience much more bearable. I will always be grateful to you. And to my nieces and nephews, (my future doctors), a special thank you for all your prayers in your own little child-like ways. My gratitude to all my friends, brothers and sisters in Christ. One of the great realizations that comes when a disaster hits is how good and faithful friends can be. I will never be able to adequately thank my parish priest Father Tom Vandenberg, the Hofmans, the Jafaris, Richard and Nina Newell, Stella Iwuoha and family, Michele and Suzie, Julia, Dr. Lee and family, Dr. Chris Adekoya and family, the Englunds, Dr. Onyali and family, Deshanel, the Magbalatas, the Berkels, Sandy, Gloria, Deirdre and Deanna, ... the list goes on. And to all my other friends, brothers and sisters in Christ, thank you for all the hundreds of get well cards, masses, prayers, emails and phone calls. I personally read all your cards and emails. Thank you very much. To my doctors, nurses, attendants, aides and technicians, thank you for taking very good care of me and for your kindness and dedication. I will forever be grateful to these generous people for the rest of my life. Finally, but not the least, I want to thank Father Jim Northrop - my spiritual director for coming to anoint me at the hospital and for all his prayers and masses.

Dedication
This Book Is Dedicated To Daddy And Mummy, John And Grace Egbejimba In Thanksgiving To God For Their Wonderful Gift Of Good Christian Values To Me And My Siblings.
God Bless You Two! Amen.

PREFACE

Dear brothers and sisters in Christ, there is a saying in Igbo - a Nigerian language - "Echi dime, Onyema ihe agamu echi" "Tomorrow is pregnant ... who knows what will be delivered tomorrow." This saying made more sense to us over fifty years ago when we did not have all the advancements that we have now in medicine. In those days, when you get pregnant, you live your pregnancy months, one day at a time. There were no pregnancy tests to confirm that you are indeed pregnant with a baby. You could be pregnant with a tumor or something else. There were no ultrasounds to tell you the sex of the baby.

You are pregnant, and because no body but God really knows the outcome of this pregnancy, you go one day at a time for the next forty weeks. You could not even have a baby shower. You waited until the delivery of the baby to celebrate the baby. Those were the good old days of being pregnant, when every single day of your pregnancy was seen as a gift, and every precious moment treasured.

So how should we live our lives? Life is a precious gift from God, and we should treasure each precious moment that is given to us. We should be thankful and very appreciative of every single second of every single minute of the day. We should learn to enjoy, relish, appreciate and cherish today. We should stay in the present time zone - in the now. We take so many things for granted these days and this is not right. We are so busy doing things that we seem to have forgotten how to be human beings. I used to be very busy with my daily 'things to do' list, but not any more. My illness and hospitalization taught me a very big lesson, and I thank God for the "new and improved" me! They say the line between life and death is paper thin, but I think it is thinner than that.

I will never complain about anything again, even the weather. For ten good days, I was hospitalized, not able to witness our unpredictable weather changes. You know it is a privilege to witness the beautiful sunshine disappear into the clouds, giving way to the graceful Seattle rain in a matter of minutes. Let us take time each day to thank God for everything and for everyone in our lives. Let us take time everyday to hug our loved ones, and take time to tell them how much we love them. Let us take time daily to thank the cashier at the grocery store (instead of complaining about how slow he/she is), the bank teller, our teachers, pastors, friends, co-workers, bosses, coaches, employees, employers, students, doctors, nurses, patients, customers, clients, janitors, associates, relatives and even the in-laws we cannot stand. Let us take time daily to smell the roses and enjoy God's beautiful work of creation. Remember, tomorrow is very pregnant, and no one knows.

The first part of this book contains my personal story through the dark valley of death. The second part of the book consists of the dream I had three weeks before my illness, and my reflections on the scripture the good Lord gave me after the dream - Ephesians chapter 6, verses 10 - 18. My message is personal but yet it is applicable to every Christian life. As you read this book, "I pray that the God of our Lord Jesus Christ, the Father of Glory, may give you a spirit of wisdom and revelation as you come to know him, so that, with the eyes of your heart enlightened, you may know what is the hope to which he has called you, what are the riches of his glorious inheritance among the saints." Amen. (Ephesians 1:17-18). All Scriptural references are to The New Revised Standard Version (Catholic Edition).

Love and prayers - Stella Ihuoma Nnanabu

INTRODUCTION

Once, while serving as a deacon in Southern California during my last year in the seminary, a woman approached me after Mass while we were having coffee and said she wanted to share something with me. I invited her to be seated next to me and she mentioned how she enjoyed my referencing the Psalm of the day which was Psalm 23 during my homily. Then she asked me a question.

She said, "Which word in that Psalm has the greatest importance?" I thought for a moment, and said, "They are all important. What do you mean?"

This woman then proceeded to tell me that the most important word was "through." I looked puzzled but she went on to explain that the Psalm didn't say, "Even *though* I walk *around, over, below,* or *past the valley of darkness*", but rather, "even though I walk through the valley of darkness I fear no evil." She then told me about her life and how the Lord had taught her that walking faithfully as a Christian didn't mean a life free from trials as many televangelists and self-help Christian books would suggest, but that life is filled with trials and the one promise you can always bank on is that God will lead you with "his hand on your shoulder and his rod to guide you." (cf. Psalm 23) She described her own life which was filled with difficulties and challenges but also filled with tremendous gratitude for the faithfulness God had shown her. I was totally impressed and thought this was a mature Christian woman.

Little was I expecting to encounter such a profound witness to the power of Jesus Christ while sipping my coffee after Mass.

Suffering always tests our faith but it also forges our faith and allows us to joyfully proclaim with St. Paul that it is possible to "do all things through Christ who strengthens us." (cf. Philippians 4:13)

The following pages you are about to read contain a powerful testimony to the power of God's grace which shines gloriously through adversity. Stella Ihuoma Nnanabu has written a beautiful testimony that I know will inspire and give you courage through any trials you may be facing or will face in the future. She also shares practical spiritual advice that will build up your understanding of Scripture and how to stand firmly as a witness to the power of the Cross of Jesus Christ. I have gotten to know Stella over the years and feel incredibly blessed to know her.

St. Paul also shared his advice with us in his letter to the Colossians: "I am now rejoicing in my sufferings for your sake, and in my flesh I am completing what is lacking in Christ's afflictions for the sake of his body, that is, the church. I became its servant according to God's commission that was given to me for you, to make the word of God fully known, the mystery that has been hidden throughout the ages and generations but has now been revealed to his saints. To them God chose to make known how great among the gentiles are the riches of the glory of this mystery, which is Christ in you, the hope of glory. It is he whom we proclaim, warning everyone and teaching everyone in all wisdom, so that we may present everyone mature in Christ. For this I toil and struggle with all the energy that he powerfully inspires within me." (Colossians 1: 24 - 29) May all of us discover in our struggles and toils that God's divine power is at work within us. St. John declared

"For the one who is in you is greater than the one who is in the world." (1 John 4:4)

Rev. Fr. Jim Northrop

Spiritual Director, Western Washington Catholic Charismatic Renewal

FOREWORD

Dear Reader,

In the Christian community, testimonies are very important. I like testimonies because they alert me to the ways that God manifests himself in my life as well as the lives of my brothers and sisters in Christ. Often God manifests his love in our lives by what unbelievers call "coincidences." My friend used to say to unbelievers, "When I pray, coincidences happen. When I stop praying, coincidences stop happening." For the Christian there are no coincidences. Our Father's loving providence is revealed in sickness and in health and in what seem to be chance encounters. We shall all face serious trials at some point in our lives. Stella's testimony has helped me to prepare for that point in my life. Her use of Scripture is apt and powerful. This book will help you to "Be strong in the Lord and in the strength of his power." (Ephesians 6:10). We are well advised, "Put on the whole armor of God, so that you may be able to stand against the wiles of the devil." (Ephesians 6:11)

Yours in Christ,

Rev (Dr.) Fr. Bob W. Dundon, S.J. Omaha, Nebraska

PSALM TWENTY-THREE - THE DIVINE SHEPHERD

The LORD is my shepherd; I shall not want.
He makes me lie down in green pastures,
He leads me besides still waters,
He restores my soul.
He leads me in right paths
For his name's sake.
Even though I walk **THROUGH THE Darkest VALLEY,**
I fear no evil,
for you are with me;
your rod and your staff,
they comfort me.
You prepare a table before me
in the presence of my enemies.
You anoint my head with oil;
my cup overflows.
Surely goodness and mercy shall follow me
all the days of my life,
and I shall dwell in the house of the LORD; my whole life
long.

PART ONE

My Hospitalization And Experience
In The Dark Valley Of Death...

CHAPTER ONE
No Pain No Gain

The day was Wednesday, December 29th 2004, and we all - Jerry, myself, and our three kids went to the Wednesday evening mass. Because familiarity breeds contempt, I have made it a point to receive every Holy Communion as my first one, (with all the joy and anticipation), as my only one, and also as my last one, (with all the appreciation and thankfulness.) This without knowing it, would have been my last Holy Communion.

The next day, Thursday, December 30th was also a very busy day. I went out, ran some errands, and came back that evening tired. I am a very organized working mother of three wonderful kids and a wife to my boy friend of nineteen years, so I am a very busy woman. Being very organized, I always have my week planned ahead of time. I have already lost the virtue to treasure and relish each precious day of my life. This is what happens when you are too busy; you end up being a calendar yourself. The days zoom by so fast that all you remember in a year are New Year's Day, Easter, Thanksgiving Day, and O my goodness, it's Christmas again!

A year has just flown by. You tend to forget to slow down, to smell the roses. New Year's Eve came by, I went out again and finished my to-do list for the day (Praise God!). I was able to crash into Top Food three minutes before closing, rushed home, and marinated my turkey for New Year's Day. I baked some corn bread and lemon cake for the New Year's Day. Before I knew it, it was 10:30 PM already, and my daughter would die (literally) if she did not watch the count down on TV at 12 midnight. So, we all gathered around our altar, said the rosary and had our last family meeting for the year. We re-emphasized our family values, set our family goals for 2005, and re-dedicated ourselves to the sacred heart of Jesus and the immaculate heart of Mary. Oh no, couple more minutes to 12 midnight, and we all rushed to our bedroom to watch the count down on TV at 12 midnight. After this, we celebrated, hugged and kissed each other, and shared some bottles of apple cider. Then it was time to call our family members to wish them a happy New-year. Finally, we all settled down to watch a movie together. At about 2:00 AM, I announced to Jerry and the kids that I was signing off for the night because I was feeling sleepy. The big warning was that "New Year's mass is at 9:00 AM and I have set the alarm for 7:45 AM". We will be at mass to start the New Year with the Holy Mass as we have always done in past years.

At about 3:00 AM, I woke up with a tummy ache. I woke Jerry up and he told me to go sit on the toilet to see if I could have a bowel movement. About thirty minutes later, Jerry rushed into the restroom because he heard me screaming on top of my lungs. Jerry in his usual calm way bent over to pat my shoulder, but I immediately pushed his hand away. I was in an excruciating pain, and the pain was radiating to every single fiber of my body. I continued screaming for another hour or so. Jerry suggested that we should go to the Emergency room, but I refused because I thought I was having an intestinal flu. At about 4:30 AM, I started to throw up. After about another hour of screaming and throwing up, Jerry drove me to the Emergency room. I made a joke to Jerry that the news headline would have read "A healthy mother of three dies in her bathroom after a serious abdominal pain." This news headline will not sound good in the newspapers.

When we got to the hospital at about 6:30 AM, I was in a worst pain than I was before I left home. The Emergency room nurses were very friendly, fast and quick. When the doctor walked in, I was screaming of pain and pain! She asked me, "On a scale of 1 to 10, 10 being the worst, where is your pain?" I looked at her in a daze and cried out "12!" She asked if I was allergic to any medications, and I replied that I am allergic to morphine. Immediately, an IV was started with all the strong pain medications. By now, my tummy was very much distended. The nurses and doctor talked with my husband to get a history of my illness. The first X-ray showed some gas and a lot of fecal matter in my tummy. Then the result of the first Cat-scan also came back inconclusive, only showing some gas and a lot of fecal matter in my tummy.

After five hours of receiving continuous strong IV pain medications, I was sent home. The doctor instructed me to be on clear liquid diet for the rest of the day, and to come back if the pain gets bad again. When we got home, I crashed on the bed for a nap. When I got up at about 2:00 PM, my kids were in my bedroom praying for me. I had a sip of water, (truly just a sip of water), and the nightmare started again, this time in a big way. On the pain scale of one to ten, my pain had gone up to thirteen. I started to throw up again and my tummy was now getting distended again. Jerry whisked me off to the Emergency room. When we got to the Emergency room this time, you would think they were having an after Christmas sale and every merchandise was one hundred percent off. Yes, one hundred percent off! The Emergency room was packed, it seemed like every body was there for one reason or the other. We even met some friends from our church.

After three hours of screaming and throwing up, I finally got to see the doctor. By this time, my pain on the famous pain scale was at fourteen, my tummy looked like I was six to eight months pregnant, and I was throwing up like crazy. Same old strong pain medication, and anti-vomiting medication, and a second Cat-scan with a contrast dye were given to me. The Cat-scan came back also inconclusive. Don't you love that? You are dying and nobody with all our medical and scientific advances knows what is killing you. They ran a battery of blood and urine tests and every single test came back normal. Jerry and I continued to pray. I told him another joke. I told him that I have changed the Newspaper headline to read: "A crazy mother of three dies in the Emergency room after hours of excruciating abdominal pain of unknown cause." I have to be crazy because if all the X-rays, Cat-scans, blood and urine tests came back with normal results, then the pain must be in my head. The Emergency room doctor this time was very gracious. Thank God! He said "Stella I am worried about the cause of your pain, I will not let you go home, I will keep you here over night, but the only problem is that we do not have a single vacant bed in all the floors for you. So you will have to spend the night here in the Emergency room, until we can find a bed for you." At this point, I said to myself, "I knew it, what a weird place for an after Christmas clearance sale - the hospital, am I glad I didn't miss it this year". At around 1:00 AM, I begged Jerry to go home back to my three angels. My poor kids with so many aunties, uncles and cousins, everybody was calling the house on New Year's day wanting to speak to us, "Where is your mother?" "In the hospital," they responded. "What s wrong with her?" They answered, "We do not know." Talk about dumb teenagers!

CHAPTER TWO
MORE PAIN, MORE GAIN

It was Sunday January 2nd 2005, I was busy enjoying my nice, heavily-sedated sleep, (You know the type you can never get at home with three teenage kids and a wonderful husband), when a tap woke me up. It was 10:30 AM and the nurse said "We finally have a bed for you on the first floor." I was very excited. Those Emergency room beds should be called Emergency room tables. I immediately called Jerry and left a message on his cell phone, because they were still at Sunday Mass. Around 11:15 AM, I opened my tired eyes to see three well dressed kids and a very handsome gentleman praying over me. My heart was full of joy, for "The joy of the Lord is my strength." (Nehemiah 8:10b).

The whole day was busy with visitors, phone calls, more X-rays and tests to rule out kidney stones, gall bladder stones and pancreatitis. I had appendectomy when I was in junior high so that was not a threat. Anyway, the highlight of the day was that I was given a PCA (A patient controlled Analgesia). I wonder why anyone hasn't thought about an over the counter mobile PCAs. I pressed the living day lights out of my PCA to relieve the excruciating pain. It is a smart machine though; you can only get pain medication every eight minutes no matter how many times you press it. Trust me, my eyes were on that clock, I couldn't afford to miss the next eight minutes of my pain free life.

Monday, January 3rd, - Today is my parent's forty-sixth wedding anniversary and their birthdays, too. They waited all day for my phone call and did not hear from their faithful child. They knew something was wrong - even Jerry and the kids didn't call to wish them a happy birthday and a happy wedding anniversary. That's it. They called my brother in Alaska and finally got the news of my illness. My hospital phone rang and I picked up the phone, when I heard my dad's voice, I froze. "Oh no, I have just been caught in the very act of being sick." You see, my mom has high blood pressure and has a "PhD" degree in panicking; we were trying to hide my illness from them, just trying to avoid my mom from having a stroke or a heart attack. Instantly my excruciating pain disappeared, I cleared my voice. My game plan was to pretend not to be too sick, you know... pretending to be a healthy sick person. What an oxymoron. My dad said "Stella, what is wrong with you?" I answered "I have a tummy ache." He asked "What is the cause of your tummy ache?" "I do not know," I said, "What do you mean you don't know?" I answered "Because nobody else knows." Meanwhile in the background, I could hear my mom crying and sobbing. "Stella why have you decided to do this to me, do you really want me to die. Stella please don't you do this to me." My mind started reciting - "What am I doing to her?" I thought I was the sick one, with a distended "seven month like pregnant" tummy, and in a very very bad pain. What did I do? I started to cry, and my mother and I enjoyed an undisturbed synchronized crying session. While Jerry was trying to calm me down, my dad was also at the other end trying to calm my mom down. The last word I had my mom say was "Stella please don't you die, because if you die, I will die."

Have you ever felt helpless before? Satan was trying to rob me of my faith and the powerful weapon of prayer. Then

I remembered the movie, "The Passion of Christ", and how Satan tried to rob Jesus of His faith and the powerful weapon of prayer. A statement I heard on Catholic radio by Archbishop Fulton Sheen came to my mind: "Nothing is worst than wasted suffering." I started offering my pain to God for all the abortions that will be committed to-day all around the world. I asked God to use my excruciating pain for the forgiveness of sins, and also for the conversion of souls. For the purpose of our suffering must outweigh the pain. Matthew 28:20b came to my mind "And remember, I am with you always, to the end of the age." The emphasis here for me is the word "always". We have prayed for three good days but my pain kept getting worse every single day. But I refused to rely on my emotions. I relied on God's word. I agreed within myself to walk in the Spirit rather than in the flesh. You see, emotions are a Christian's worst enemy. Emotions bound a Christian to be led in the flesh instead of being led in the Spirit. Hebrews 13:5b flashed through my mind. The Lord said "I will never leave you or forsake you." I turned to God and said in my mind "I know you are a God who likes to show off. You like to invest in things that are bad. You waited till Lazarus was in the tomb for three days. When I look around in the natural, things don't make sense to me now. But I just cannot wait to see how you will turn things around for me."

The rest of the day went by with my new found video game, aka (also known as) the PCA. I couldn't stop pushing on that button. My doctor came by that evening and decided to prep me for an endoscopy for the next day. By now I should say I was almost in a septic shock. I was delirious and was told that I was talking garbage. My kidneys and my urinary tract were failing and they had to pass a Foley catheter to take care of urination. Also a Naso-gastric tube was passed through my nose, and this experience was everything but pleasant. My beloved husband Jerry started making fun of me, calling me "Pinocchio nose" because of the naso-gastric tube protruding out of my nose. Very funny indeed Jerry!

Anyway, the prep for the endoscopy involved a ducolax suppository, a laxative and the flushing of the gastro-intestinal tract with a gallon of "Golitely". The whole idea is to cleanse the intestines of any fecal matter, so that the doctor can have a nice time scoping through my stomach and my intestines. After the ducolax suppository, the laxative and a gallon of the Golitely, I was not passing any stool or gas, and this was very unusual. My tummy now looks like a nine month old pregnant tummy. The doctor knew that something was wrong, but what? They decided to suction the fecal matter, (stool), from my nose through the naso-gastric tube. This was a real dejavu. This reminded me of back home in Nigeria when the septic tank guy came once a year to suction our septic tanks.

After about three big tubs of stool were suctioned out of me, the doctor decided to stop and take one more X-ray. The day was Tuesday morning, January 4th, 2005. I was wheeled to the X-ray room for the hundredth time (who is counting!). This time a partial obstruction of the small intestine was found on the X-rays. "Praise God". I shouted. I was ecstatic. I turned to Jerry and made another joke. "Thank God the news headline will not say that she died of unknown causes". The X-ray was immediately followed by another Cat-scan with a contrast dye. The result of the Cat-scan was very conclusive - a complete obstruction of the lower right quadrant of my small intestine, Alleluia! After four painful days we finally know what is wrong with me.

I never for once asked - Why me Lord?" (Never!) "Why not me?" I was in terrible pain, very uncomfortable with a very

very distended tummy, but I had peace. You know that peace of God that surpasses all understanding. It was amazing. Jerry was very calm, peaceful and prayerful. He was communicating the whole time with my brother-in-law, Dr. Casmir Okoro who is in Atlanta. My mom, dad, children, sisters, brothers, sisters and brothers-in-law, cousins, aunties, uncles, nieces, nephews, friends and co-workers were all pounding the gates of heaven with their fervent prayers. My sister Lilian called my spiritual director, Rev Fr. Jim Northrop to come and give me the anointing of the sick. Father Jim Northrop came, anointed me, and prayed for me. "Even though I walk through the darkest valley, I fear no evil, for you are with me, your rod and your staff - they comfort me. You prepare a table before me in the presence of my enemies, you **ANOINT MY HEAD WITH OIL**, and my cup overflows." (Psalm 23: 4 - 5).

CHAPTER THREE
THE SURGERY AND RECOVERY

The time was 7:15 PM, Tuesday, January 4th, 2005; the surgeon just walked in and was consulting with us. He was very thorough, and explained to Jerry and I why we do not need to jump into surgery immediately. He suggested that we should continue with the suctioning of the stool from my tummy for a day or two, hoping that the obstruction might be cleared as has been the case in most patients. He suggested that by tomorrow Wednesday or by Thursday, if I wasn't feeling any better, then we will go into surgery. You see the Cat-Scan showed that there was a complete obstruction, but did not show the cause of the obstruction and the severe pain. Finally the surgeon wanted to examine my tummy and I reached out and grabbed his hands and told him in a very firm voice that he couldn't touch me because I was in so much pain. He smiled and said "Ok, would you let go of my hand now". Then I let go of his hands. As he was about to leave the room at 8:00 PM he turned around and asked "Any more questions?" Jerry said "Yes, what if there is a gangrenous tissue?" This was a Holy Spirit moment! The surgeon's facial countenance fell, he stepped out to call the operating room and the anesthesiologist on call was there. He walked back into my room and announced that "We are going into surgery in thirty minutes." Jerry signed all the consent forms and he had time to pray with me. He kissed me and walked away. He was at peace and I was at peace. As I was wheeled into the operating room, I started reading Romans 8: 37-39 in my mind: "No, in all these things we are more than conquerors through him who loved us. For I am convinced that neither death nor life, nor angels, nor rulers, nor things present, nor things to come, nor powers, nor height, nor depth, nor anything else in all creation, will be able to separate us from the love of God in Christ Jesus our Lord." Wow, nothing can beat this. This is one of my favorite scripture verses.

Surgery lasted for about two hours and was very successful. Praise be to Jesus! The next day was Wednesday, January 5th. When I woke up, the first thing I noticed was that my roses were on the right side of the room instead of the left side. I asked my nurse who moved my roses, and she explained to me that I had surgery last night and that I am in the ICU (intensive care unit). The showers of roses deserve to be detailed and I will discuss them later. Then I started counting the number of heart monitor wires, IV lines, tubes, cords all around me and I exclaimed "Praise the Lord I am hooked on phonics." My heart rate was very high, (136) - double the normal rate. My temperature was also very high - over 104 degrees centigrade. But all in all I felt great. My pain was completely gone. I sat up that day and miraculously walked around with the help of the nurses. The doctor walked into my room that Wednesday morning and asked Jerry my husband to have a seat. He said, "Thank God we went into surgery last night, if we had waited one more day, Stella would have been history." He went on to say that my case was a very bizarre and unusual case, once in a life time type of case. My right ovary wrapped around my small intestine and strangulated it, cutting it off from blood supply and nutrient. Ninety centimeters (three feet) of my small intestine was dead and gangrenous (Remember the Holy Spirit moment before surgery, when Jerry asked the doctor "What if there is a gangrenous tissue?")

This dead and gangrenous ninety centimeters of my small intestine was cut off and the intestine was resutured together. Jerry and I looked at each other in utmost shock. I said "Thank God He still wants me here, and there must be a reason for that." I don't know why but Romans 8:28 explains why: "We know that all things work together for good for those who love God, who are called according to his purpose." - You see, the Almighty God works through all things to bring good to His people. Note that this verse does not say that God causes all things that happen to us. God is a good righteous and faithful God who does not cause evil and suffering. In His sovereignty, He does permit them and He intends to use them for good even when Satan means them for bad. This verse does not teach that all things that happen to us are good, but it does teach us that when evil things happen to us, that God can work through these evil circumstances to bring a blessing to His people. We may suffer, but we need not lose faith or despair.

Recovery was really very miraculous through God's grace. God is a very faithful father; He always finishes what He starts very well. He said in Exodus 15:26 "I am the Lord who heals you." I spent three days in ICU and was moved to the regular surgical floor.

The Quest for Gas

Two days after surgery, the quest for gas began. I started flashing a twenty dollar bill for anyone who could help me pass gas. The next day, I started flashing a fifty dollar bill. By Saturday, four days after the surgery, I was offering a hundred dollar bill. I sounded like an auctioneer to the highest bidder, Going! Going!! Gas!!! It was exactly 8:45 AM and I screamed

"Praise God" I picked up the phone and called Jerry and all my family members to announce the discovery of this new wonder gas experience. It was one "Praise the Lord" after the other. Who ever knew that passing gas could call for so much celebration and a praiseworthy event? I will never take anything for granted again in life.

The Foley Folly

After I passed gas, things started changing for the better for me. The finest gadget I was most happy to lose was my Pinocchio nose - the naso-gastric tube. Next to follow was the Foley catheter. It was very important for me to go pee within the next eight hours after the removal of the Foley catheter. But nobody warned me of what was about to happen. Two hours later, I felt pressure in my bladder to go pee. I called the nurse and announced that I would like to go pee. I stood up and as the nurse was helping me to the bathroom, the worst happened. I felt urine trickling down my thighs. "Oh no" I screamed, "I am peeing and I can't stop it." I was very embarrassed. I peed on the floor! I just had an accident, Oops! I apologized to my nurse who explained to me that it is going to take my brain some time to re-learn urination control. I had flash backs to my preschool years. I was immediately given diapers for a day or so before I regained control of my urination. Life is so funny! Very very funny!!

The next two days, January 9th and 10th went by very fast. My room turned into a praise and worship center. A lot of friends from church and from the prayer meeting group stopped by to see me, and we had some nice time praising and worshiping the Almighty Jehovah for His loving kindness and His divine mercy. I thank God for the tremendous reaction of support and prayers from my family, friends, brothers and sisters in Christ. "The prayer of the righteous is powerful and effective." (James 5:16). This does not mean that God only hears the prayers of the spiritual "SWAT'" team, but that God indeed listens to those who believe in Him and have, by their faith in Jesus, been acquitted of judgment and pronounced righteous. This is one of the great blessings of belonging to the Catholic Charismatic renewal and also to a wonderful vibrant parish family.

I was started on clear fluid diet, then full liquid diet, and then was sent home on a soft diet. The ride home was very emotional for me. I cried with joy as Jerry drove out of the hospital parking lot, stopped for a minute, praised God, and then we prayed for all the other patients we were leaving behind at the hospital. Remember this place has been home to me for the past ten days. The other patients and I were one big family and I am leaving them. I thought about the lonely patients. Some of the patients were terribly lonely. You know visiting the sick is one of the Corporal works of Mercy. I am calling on all Christians out there to make it a point of duty, out of love, to visit one sick person in the hospital or nursing home every week. Remember what Jesus told us in Matthew 25:3b "I was naked and you gave me clothing, I was sick and you took care of me, I was in prison and you visited me."

When I got home, tears filled my eyes; I wouldn't stop praising and thanking God. Jerry and I went upstairs to our altar and spent some time thanking God for the miracle of healing, and we busted out in David's praise to God:"Blessed are you, O Lord, the God of our ancestor Israel, forever and ever. Yours O Lord, are the greatness, the power, the glory, the victory, and the majesty, for all that is in the heavens and on the earth is yours, yours is the kingdom, O Lord, and you are exalted as head above all. Riches and honor come from you, and you rule over all. In your hand are power and might, and it is in your hand to make great and to give strength to all. And now, our God, we give thanks to you and praise your glorious name." (I Chronicles 29: 10-13.)

The Shower of Roses

I want to explain the shower of roses and the scent of roses I had in my room during my hospital stay. I received over a dozen vases of roses of every color and size from family and friends. My room constantly had the scent of roses in it. The nurses and aides would always come by my room just to smell the roses and they would always comment "Stella you must love roses, every body is bringing you roses." And I will just smile and say quietly to myself "Thank you big sister." You see I have a big sister in heaven and her name is Saint Therese of Lisieux. She is a very faithful and dedicated big sister, and a good role model to me. I pray with her every day and my prayer goes like this "Saint Therese, the little flower, please pick me a rose from the heavenly garden, and send it to me with a message of love. Ask God to grant me the favor I thee implore and tell him I will love him each day more and more, Amen." Born in 1873, Saint Therese entered the Carmelite convent at the tender age of fifteen. She led a quiet, obscure, humble life in the convent, recognizing that her greatest work would come later. "After my death, I will let fall a shower of roses. I will spend my heaven doing good on earth." And so it has been since her untimely death at the age of twenty four, her intercession has brought healings, miracles and blessings, many accompanied by roses or the scent of roses. She was canonized in 1925 and in 1997 Pope John Paul II declared her a "Doctor of the church" because of her tremendous spiritual legacy.

PART TWO

Waging A Spiritual Warfare
And Claiming The Victory!

INTRODUCTION TO PART TWO

Three weeks before my illness and hospitalization, I had a dream, and after the dream, the good Lord gave me Ephesians 6:10-18, which talks about the whole Armor of God. The second part of this book explains the dream and expands on my reflection on waging a spiritual warfare and claiming the victory by putting on the whole armor of God. The different components of the whole Armor of God include:

The belt of truth

The breastplate of righteousness

The shoes of readiness

The shield of faith

The helmet of salvation

The sword of the Spirit, and

Prayer

These different components of the whole Armor of God were the forces behind my victory over Satan *when I walked through the dark valley of death.*

CHAPTER FOUR
The Dream

On Wednesday December 8th 2004, I had a very vivid dream. In this dream, I ran into a group of Satan worshipers on my way home. These people were about two hundred in number. They held me and wanted to initiate me into their cult. I was shown some of the initiation dance moves and rituals. Immediately, I started praying the rosary, and I was strictly warned not to pray nor use the name of Jesus. Initially, I was not brave enough to pray my rosary loud so I was praying my rosary in my mind. After some time, I saw my dad. Apparently he heard that I have been captured and detained by some Satan worshipers and he came to rescue me. I walked over to my dad and told him to immediately sneak out through the back door of the building because he will be killed if they notice him. I assured him that I will be fine in Jesus name, and that all I needed from him and Mummy was their prayers. He left. Some few minutes later, my dad's picture was being passed around among these evil people and they were searching for my dad to kill him.

Then the ritual started, these horrible people started taking roll calls for their membership. During this roll call, members responded by calling out their numbers which indicated their ranks in the satanic army. I also witnessed a lady levitate and fly away on a mission. By now, I have summoned up enough courage and I started praying out loud. I was warned again and threatened to be killed if I pray or call the name of

Jesus. I ignored them and continued praying out louder. As I prayed the rosary, at the mention of the name Jesus, these evil people were falling to the ground around me. Then came the empowerment I needed from the Holy Spirit. Philippians 2:10 came to my mind, "So that at the name of Jesus, every knee should bend in heaven and on earth and under the earth." Praise God! Immediately I started praying out louder and louder calling the name above all names, the name of Jesus. I was pleading the blood of Jesus for deliverance of all these souls. Then the miracle started, as I prayed, people were being delivered one after the other. Before I knew it, all the people about two hundred in number, were delivered and we were all singing a song I taught then " Jesus Power- Super Power, Jesus Power - Super Power."

Out of nowhere came out a lady; she was dressed in an ethnic attire. On this outfit she had on, were over a dozen pockets of fire. This lady was the head of the satanic cult and she was very angry with me. She charged towards me to attack me and I started calling that name that is above all names, the powerful name of Jesus. I started praying in tongues. I boldly told her that I was going to disgrace her with all her satanic powers before her ex-members. I continued praying in tongues and before every body who was present; this lady was reduced to a smothering pot of smoke. I turned to the crowd and in glory and thanksgiving to God we began again to sing "Jesus power - Super Power! Jesus power - Super Power!!." Then I woke up from my dream in a pool of water. I was wet from sweating. I got up and I knelt down in prayer, and woke Jerry up to pray for me and with me. I thanked God that it was just a dream, because the dream was very vivid that I thought everything that was happening was real. During my prayer that night after the dream, the Lord gave me Ephesians 6:10 - 18, "The Whole armor of God."

FORCES OF EVIL AND HUMAN SUFFERING

Ephesians 6: 10 - 12 says: "Finally, be strong in the Lord and in the strength of his power. Put on the whole armor of God, so that you may be able to stand against the wiles of the devil. For our struggle is not against enemies of blood and flesh, but against the rulers, against the authorities, against the cosmic powers of the present darkness, against the spiritual forces of evil in heavenly places."

The dream and what it all meant started being real to me after my illness. The Lord, I believe, is calling me into a type of a deliverance ministry. I discussed the dream with my best friend Jerry, and a few Christian friends and I asked them to pray for me. I asked God to use me wherever He seems fit. There is a prayer I say every morning. It's John Neumann's meditation written on March 7th 1848. A portion of it goes like this: "O Emmanuel, O Sapientia, I give myself to thee. I trust thee wholly. Thou are wiser than I, more loving to me than I myself. Deign to fulfill thy high purposes in me, whatever they be, work in and through me. I am born to serve thee, to be thine, to be thy instrument. Let me be thy blind instrument, I ask not to see, I ask not to know, I ask simply to be used."

Dear brothers and sisters, Satan and his forces are real. Some very good Christians believe that God is real, but unfortunately they have a hard time acknowledging the presence of Satan and his army. Many Christians would prefer not to talk about Satan, feeling that talking about Satan will some how bring him glory. While others are so afraid of him, they say that if they ignore him, he will go away. Still others don't want to admit his existence and possible threat to the believer.

As Christians, we must struggle with super human forces of evil, including Satan. The enemy causing the evil we sometimes face is not a human force that we have a chance to defeat in our own power. The enemy includes rulers, authorities, powers, angelic forces, thrones and dominions created by God through Christ, who have rebelled against God and exercise temporary power in our universe. Colossians 1:16 tells us "For in him all things in heaven and on earth were created, things visible and invisible, whether thrones, or dominions or rulers or powers - all things have been created through him and for him."

My illness was noting but a satanic attack. What in the world was my right ovary doing around my small intestine? The Lord wants to use me, but Satan got angry and launched an attack. God's spiritual armor helped me gain victory. So my dear brothers and sisters, will God or Satan exercise the ultimate control of our lives? Let's see what the Bible says. The Bible assures us that God's victory is guaranteed. Ephesians 1:3 says "Blessed be the God and Father of our Lord Jesus Christ, who has blessed us in Christ with every spiritual blessing in the heavenly places." Ephesians 1:20 - 22 says "God put this power to work in Christ when He raised him from the dead and seated him at his right hand in the heavenly places, far above all rulers and authority and power and dominion, and above every name that is named, not only in this age but also in the age to come. And He has put all things under his feet and has made him the head over all things for the church."

We all as Christians can participate in God's victory by identifying with God and living according to His will in all aspects of our lives.

CHAPTER FIVE
The Whole Armor of God—The Belt of Truth

Ephesians 6:13-14a says "Therefore take up the whole armor of God, so that you may be able to withstand on that evil day, and having done everything, to stand firm. Stand therefore, and fasten the belt of truth around your waist." Why the belt? - When Saint Paul wrote to the Ephesians, he was chained to one of Caesar's guards. So he used a Roman soldier's armor and weapons to illustrate to us his points. The most important part of the Roman soldier's armor was the belt. It was six to eight inches wide, and the soldier attached his whole armor and weapons to it. If his belt slipped in battle, he would become very vulnerable. All our combat equipment stands or falls with our belt of truth. A solider does not wait until he was already in a battle to put on his belt. What is the Truth? - The truth of who you are as a child of God. The truth that you have been empowered by God. "See I have given you authority to tread on snakes and scorpions, and over all the power of the enemy and nothing will hurt you." (Luke 10:19). This verse is not a call to Christians to test God by opening themselves to danger. It is a call to know God's power and victory over all that opposes them. "Little children, you are from God and have conquered them, for the one who is in you is greater than the one who is in the world." (1John 4:4). Yes, no body, no evil spirit can intimidate us. There is God's power on the inside of us. We have to know this truth and draw on His power within us. Not only have we been empowered by God, but He is still empowering us today, tomorrow and forever. Knowing this truth of who we are, makes us to have a different mind set. God is the power that is beyond all comprehension. The truth is that "I can do all things through him who strengthens me." (Philippians 4:13)

The truth of the source of this power is the Holy Eucharist. We have to believe in the truth of the real and substantial presence of Jesus in the Holy Eucharist. Let's go to John 6:22-69. Jesus bluntly said: "I am the living bread that came down from heaven. Whoever eats of this bread will live forever, and the bread that I will give for the life of the world is my flesh." (Verse 51). Jesus' words sent the whole crowd arguing and quarreling among themselves.

"How can this man give us his flesh to eat." (Verse 52). The confusion and arguing among the crowd is understandable. Jesus' teaching and words sounded repulsive and cannibalistic. But guess what? Jesus was bent on emphasizing on His real and substantial presence in the Holy Eucharist. "Very truly, I tell you, unless you eat the flesh of the son of man, and drink his blood, you have no life in you. Those who eat my flesh and drink my blood have eternal life, and I will raise them up on the last day, for my flesh is true food and my blood true drink. Those who eat my flesh and drink my blood abide in me, and I in them. Just as the living Father send me, and I live because of the Father, so whoever eats me will live because of me. This is the bread that came down from heaven, not like that which your ancestors ate, and they died. But the one who eats this bread will live forever." (Verses 53-58). Jesus absolutely refused to compromise His teaching, even when many of His own disciples complained, "This teaching is difficult, who can accept it." (Verse 60b). He fired back at His disciples by saying "Does this offend you?" (Verse 61). Jesus knew that the importance of believing in His real and substantial presence in the Eucharist can never be over emphasized. Many of His disciples left Him because He refused to compromise His teaching, (verse 66). Those disciples who left Jesus were people of weak faith who were not prepared to accept His teachings based on faith.

But the twelve apostles did not leave Him. Their faith in Jesus was very strong, and so too was their love for Him. "Lord to whom can we go? You have the words of eternal life. We have come to believe and know that you are the Holy One of God." This was Peter speaking on behalf of the other apostles in answer to the question Jesus asked, "Do you also wish to go away?" (Verse 67). You see, the twelve apostles knew Jesus very well. Their strong faith in Him led them to accept and believe His words - just based on faith.

This teaching by Jesus on His real and substantial presence in the Eucharist was a prelude to His institution of the sacrament of the Blessed Eucharist at the Last Supper. So, at the last supper, when Jesus took the loaf of bread, and the cup of wine, after blessing them and giving thanks, gave them to His apostles and said "Take, eat, this is my body, drink from it, all of you, for this is my blood of the covenant, which is poured out for many for the forgiveness of sins." (Matthew 26:26 - 27), the apostles believed Him. They believed that the bread (although still in the physical form of bread), was changed into His true flesh and the wine (although still in the physical form of wine) was changed into His true blood. Their belief in transubstantiation was strong and confirmed.

When we receive Jesus in the Holy Eucharist, we receive Him in all His greatness, His power, glory, majesty, splendor, strength and honor. We as Catholics sometimes do not comprehend very well who we receive in the Holy Eucharist.

We receive the Healer Himself, the king Himself, the Blesser Himself. Once you know the Blesser, you will never run out of blessings. You don't have a resource, you have the source. I have learned through my past experiences to seek the God of healing and not the healing of God, because once you have and know the Healer, healing becomes automatic. I have learned to seek the king, and not worry about the kingdom, because the kingdom and all the kingdom blessings will be automatic once I know the king. To know God in the Holy Eucharist is to know God intimately.

We need to know the truth in the Sacrament of reconciliation. Matthew 3:5 - 6 says "The people of Jerusalem and all Judea were going out to him, and all the region along the Jordan, and they were baptized by Him in the river Jordan, confessing their sins." Acts 19:18 says "Also many of those who became believers confessed and disclosed their practices." Jesus gave his apostles the power to forgive sin when He said "Peace be with you. As the Father has sent me so I send you". When He had said this He breathed on them and said to them, "Receive the Holy Spirit. If you forgive the sins of any, they are forgiven them; if you retain the sins of any they are retained." (John 20: 21 - 23).

For me the Sacrament of reconciliation is a time when humility takes over my pride. I go and confess my sins to a priest, a representative of God and of His Divine mercy. I receive God's mercy and forgiveness. I feel relieved, forgiven, courageous and confident that God is with me in this warfare. I receive graces from God to avoid sin and all the occasions of sin. Let me explain what I mean by occasions of sin. Occasions of sin are those circumstances in our lives that make us very vulnerable to sin. These circumstances are very unique and different for every person. What might be an occasion of sin for me might not be an occasion of sin for you. So as individuals, we need to identify those circumstances that are unique to us. This is very important if we need to avoid sin. You see Satan knows you very well and knows exactly how you tick. He will relentlessly work very hard to get you into those situations that make you vulnerable to sin. Therefore, we have to be on guard. Peter warns us in 1 Peter 5:8 "Discipline yourselves, keep alert. Like a roaring lion your adversary the devil prowls around, looking for someone to devour." Saint Paul tells us in 2 Corinthians 2:11, that Satan is very predictable. "And we do this so that we may not be outwitted by Satan for we are not ignorant of his designs."

Avoiding the occasions of sin could mean hanging up the phone, leaving a group of friends in the middle of a conversation that involves a gossip. It could mean turning off the computer or the TV. What ever it takes, you will have to physically detach yourself from the particular situation. Sometimes, when it is impossible for me to physically leave the situation, I pray in my mind. Ephesians 4:27 warns us, "And do not make room for the devil ". Also, James 4:7 added a voice to the warning for us to "resist the devil".

We also need to know the truth of who we are as children of Mary, our Blessed Mother. As a Catholic, I do not worship Mary. I honor her because she is the mother of my Lord Jesus Christ - God the son. Mother Mary was the key person in God taking on flesh and becoming a man, and this is why I honor her so highly in my life. When I was ill in the hospital, a lot of prayer chains were formed for me both here on earth and also in heaven. If I could ask my friends to pray for me, you cannot stop me from asking my Mother Mary who is in heaven to also pray for me. Just think about it, whose prayers do you think will be answered faster? Mother Mary talking to her son Jesus in heaven, or my friends who are on earth talking to Jesus?

Read about the saints. All of them had a devotion to Mary. Even our late Pope John Paul II dedicated his life completely to our Blessed Mother Mary. If you don't have a devotion to our Blessed Mother Mary, cultivate one today. Start your devotion by praying and meditating on the rosary today. The rosary is a very powerful prayer of intercession. I call it "Satan choker." When we pray the rosary, we are asking Mary, the mother of God to intercede for us both now and at the hour of our death. Through the rosary, we revisit with Mary through the life of Jesus as we reflect on the different "mysteries". These mysteries consist of four groups - Joyful, Sorrowful, Glorious and Luminous. If you already pray the rosary daily, thank God for that. If you have never prayed the rosary before, start today. Make time to pray and meditate on the rosary daily. If you commute to work everyday, guess what? You could pray the rosary on your way to or from work. The importance of the daily family rosary can never be over emphasized. In my family, 11:00 PM every day is our family rosary time, and it does not matter where we are. We have said the rosary at the airport, in the parks, while waiting for tour buses. The kids did not find it funny at the time, but they have grown to love Mother Mary and now have a devotion to her. Remember a family that prays the rosary together stays together. Start a devotion to our Blessed Mother today and you will be amazed of the transformation you will notice in all aspects of your life.

CHAPTER SIX
THE BREASTPLATE OF RIGHTEOUSNESS

Ephesians 6:14b says "And put on the breastplate of righteousness." Why the breastplate? The breastplate covers several vital organs of the body - the heart, the lungs, the liver, the spleen, the stomach, the intestines, the pancreas and the gall bladder. They are all very essential organs needed for your physical body to function properly. Have you ever wondered why the police officers and the military men and women wear bullet proof vest? It is for the same reason of protecting these essential organs. So it is with our spiritual body too, the essential vital organs need to be protected from the attacks of the evil one. The Roman soldier's breastplate was made of bronze backed with tough pieces of leather. This protected the soldier's most essential organs. If a blow got through in this area, it was fatal. So our spiritual vital organs are guarded by the certainty of the righteousness of God.

What is Righteousness? Righteousness is a visible witness to those around us that we are living a life in God through the power of the Holy Spirit, and when we fail, we repent immediately. Unless we are slaves to righteousness, we will be slaves to Satan and sin. Christians should commit themselves as slaves to God's righteousness, and then fight against sin and its temptations. Through Christ's righteous act, we are transformed by devoting our lives to the righteous way of life He pioneered. "For just as by the one man's disobedience the many were made sinners, so by the one man's obedience the many will be made righteous." (Romans 5:19). Therefore, our lives should mirror God's holiness and we will receive eternal life as God's gracious wage. Holiness should be the life style of God's people.

Holiness is our destiny. We have been called to be holy because God is Holy. Saint Peter tells us this in 1Peter 1:15, "Instead as He who called you is holy, be holy yourselves in all your conduct." Holiness means "Separation to God for His use." Christians have been separated to God on the inside, but we have to act out that separation so it can be seen on the outside, and this is what righteousness is all about. You now see the relationship between holiness and righteousness. We have been commanded to be holy in all our conducts. So let's live from inside out.

God told us in Mark 1:11, how well He is pleased with Jesus, "You are my son, the Beloved with you I am well pleased." God expects us to live to please Him just as Jesus did. There is no reason why we cannot, if we have been filled with the same Holy Spirit, and have been given His righteousness. We should be able to please God just as Jesus did.

Righteousness is walking right before God. It is a process, and we learn by practice. It takes some effort and determination. Living a righteous life does not come easy. It involves a crucifying of the flesh and doing what pleases God. Crucifying the flesh is making your flesh do something it doesn't want to do. Let us all hunger and thirst after righteousness. Let us dedicate ourselves to doing what pleases God even when it is uncomfortable to our flesh. God is calling each and everyone of us to go beyond just "not sinning" into a higher and deeper spiritual life that is pleasing to Him.

Our righteousness comes through our faith in Christ.

Christ as the sinless suffering servant, counts His righteousness as ours. Christ did not sin. He chose to die on the cross and accepted the punishment of our sins. He has given us His righteousness which includes moral righteousness and right relationship with God. "For our sake he made him to be sin who knew no sin, so that in him we might become the righteousness of God." (2 Corinthians 5:21). Jesus loves you, and paid a high price for you. Honor him with your righteous life style. This righteousness is not static, but is known for its application to both personal and social behavior. We cannot be righteous by our own efforts apart from Christ. We cannot receive righteousness from Christ without faith. Philippians 3:9, says "… and be found in him, not having a righteousness of my own that comes from the law, but one that comes through faith in Christ, the righteousness from God based on faith."

We cannot be counted as righteous in Christ without the desire to let the Spirit create a life of righteous acts in us. Only the Holy Spirit can clean up our hearts and empower us to live the kind of life God approves. A person is righteous before God when the person meets the demands of the relationship with God. So, righteousness means to meet the demands of a relationship. It is not something we claim rewards for achieving. It is God's gift in Christ through the Spirit for the people of faith. Because we are clothed with God's own righteousness, we are accepted in the beloved. "In righteousness you shall be established, you shall be far from oppression, for you shall not fear, and from terror, for it shall not come near you." (Isaiah 54:14). To be established in righteousness is to be in a right place with God. So when you put on that breastplate of righteousness, you are in a right place with God. And once you are in a right place with God, you won't be afraid to boldly stand against the flaming attacks of the evil one. You won't be afraid to do exploits in Jesus name. Then you will have that courage you need to be a soldier of Christ, and you will live in victory everyday. Saint Paul charged Timothy to "pursue righteousness", and to "fight the good fight of faith." (1Timothy 6:11 - 12). God is calling us to do the same!

CHAPTER SEVEN
THE SHOES OF READINESS

Ephesians 6:15 says "As shoes for your feet put on whatever will make you ready to proclaim the gospel of peace." Any soldier will tell you the importance of having a shoe that gives sure footing. The Roman soldier wore hobnail sandals so that he could keep a sure footing. When you are fighting with swords, your first slip is usually your last one. Sure footing can never be over-emphasized in our battle with the devil. It is very important, for the devil knows how we tick and will surely take advantage of any slip that throws us off balance. For us, our sure footing in this spiritual warfare comes from a previous preparation of the good news concerning peace. This is that inner peace that God gives us in the midst of trails - that peace that surpasses all understanding.

Philippians 4:4 - 7 tells us "Rejoice in the Lord always again I will say, Rejoice. Let your gentleness be known to everyone. The Lord is near. Do not worry about anything, but in everything by prayer and supplication with thanksgiving let your requests be made known to God. And the peace of God, which surpasses all understanding, will guard your hearts and your minds in Christ Jesus." Saint Paul is calling us to rejoice in the Lord always, not sometimes when the going is good. We are also supposed to be full of thanksgiving towards God. Such attributes bring the sense of fulfillment and joy in God that affects all our relationships and circumstances. This is God's peace, a peace so wonderful, the human mind cannot fully understand it. This peace is a present reality for the person who gently and kindly lives life by letting God take care of his/her anxieties.

Apart from the peace Jerry and I felt during those dark days when I was in the hospital, I want to share with you another experience we went through as a couple recently and how the peace of God saw us through. It was 11:00 PM on October 31, 2004, when the phone rang and it was Mr. Chris Gavin, the principal of Bellarmine Preparatory school, Tacoma, Washington. My older son, Somutoo was away on a school retreat for junior boys. The retreat was at a camp about 50 miles from Tacoma. Mr. Gavin called to inform us that Somutoo was having a hard time breathing, but Somutoo did not think it was an asthma attack. Somutoo has a fifteen year history of asthma; his last attack was over ten years ago when he was in the first grade. Apparently, he had forgotten what an asthma attack feels like. Somutoo later told me that because his inhaler was not helping him breathe better, he concluded that it must not have been an asthma attack. He actually thought he was having indigestion because he ate a lot at dinner time.

Anyway, by the time we got to the Emergency room, Somutoo was in a desperate respiratory distress. He could not breathe, so he was trying to use the muscles of the head, neck, chest, arms, back and abdomen to force some oxygen into his lungs. We felt so helpless watching our son struggling to breathe and there was nothing we could do to help him, apart from praying for him. You see prayer is the life line to that inner peace which only God can give in times of crisis. Jesus kept filling Jerry and I with this wonderful peace of His as we prayed for our son. He said in John 14:27 "Peace I leave with you my peace I give to you. I do not give to you as the world gives. Do not let your hearts be troubled and do not let them be afraid." This peace of God is not the absence of external crisis in our lives but it is the power of internal security. The drama that followed at the Emergency room is now history. Somutoo's oxygen concentration was very low. They started an IV of steroids, the flow of oxygen to the lungs through his nose and a breathing treatment with the nebulizer through his mouth. It took the doctor and nurses five good hours of continuous steroid treatment, oxygen treatment and breathing treatment to get Somutoo to a peak flow of only 150. Any thing below 300 is not good. Through it all, I did not cry nor panic. I stayed calm by God's grace and continued storming heaven with my prayers. Jesus sent the Holy Spirit to bring comfort and peace in our lives. To the Glory of God, Somutoo is till here today and looking very healthy.

God says "Be still and know that I am God!" (Psalm 46:10a). This is not easy in times of crisis and trials. Our first instinct as a human person is to try to cope with our problems in our own strength. It is very difficult to let go and simply believe the Lord. But when we do let go by letting God be God, we are then filled with that most wonderful inner peace that only God can give. The pressure and problems may still exist but there is peace inside our hearts.

The only way to have this peace of God is by believing God's promises. There are over seven thousand promises in the Bible and those are all ours to claim. We will not need these promises in heaven. They are only useful for our needs here on earth because we do not need them in heaven. Although we may be in the midst of a great spiritual warfare, we can rest inwardly and have perfect peace. No matter how great the crisis, no matter how perplexing the trials, if we learn and believe the promises of God, we can be filled with that inner peace that surpasses all understanding.

CHAPTER EIGHT
The Shield of Faith

Ephesians 6: 16 says "…with all of these, take the shield of faith, with which you will be able to quench all the flaming arrows of the evil one." The Roman soldier's shield was about two feet wide and four feet long, and it was used by the soldiers to ward off thrusts of the enemy's sword as well as arrows. The shield was the maneuverable part of the armor that covered wherever it was needed.

So what is faith? Faith is belief in and a personal commitment to Jesus Christ for eternal salvation. Faith is the maneuverable part of our Spiritual armor. It defends us against Satan's attacks of temptation, doubt, fear, anxiety, guilt, misunderstanding, sickness, false doctrine, the list goes on. Faith is a very important aspect of our relationship with God. It is the source of our strength, our guidance, our courage, our provision and our victory over Satan.

The Bible tells us that it is impossible to please God without faith; Hebrews 11:6, "And without faith, it is impossible to please God, for whoever would approach him must believe that He exists and that He rewards those who seek him." But faith is a gift of God as Romans 12:3 tells us. So God gives us this gift (called faith) without which we can not please Him. This faith we have is in God Himself. The object of our faith is God himself "By faith, he, (Abraham) received power of procreation, even though he was too old; and Sarah herself was barren; because he considered him faithful who had promised." (Hebrews 11:11), The object of Abraham's faith was God Himself - His faithfulness. Abraham was confident that God will keep His promise. The more we learn about God and maintain a consistent fellowship with Him, the more confident we are in the object of our faith - the faithfulness of God. Abraham had a personal relationship with God, in order for his knowledge and confidence in the object of his faith to grow.

You can not know some one very well unless you develop a personal relationship with that person. Without a personal relationship with God, you cannot get to know God very well, and without knowing God very well, you cannot have that assurance in the ability and faithfulness of God. Let me tell you something about my awesome husband Jerry, which I would not have known if I didn't take the time to have a personal relationship with him. Jerry is a first class cook. I have confidence in his cooking; I couldn't have known this by meeting him briefly. You see, once you develop that personal relationship with God, then you begin to see what God can do, and you also begin to trust in God's ability and faithfulness - you begin to have faith in God.

You begin to have faith in God's promises for your healing, your safety, your strength, your forgiveness, your joy, your provision, your future, your guidance, your goals, your finances, your spouse, your kids, and your victory over Satan. You begin to walk by faith and not by sight. You begin to understand the mysteries of creation and the things you do not see. "Now faith is the assurance of things hoped for, the conviction of things not seen." (Hebrews 11:1). This conviction of things not seen is best illustrated by an event that happened in the life of Elisha and his disciple Gehazi. The story is in 2 Kings 6:8-23.

The king of Aram was trying to invade Israel, but couldn't because the king of Israel knew his every plan and move beforehand. The king of Aram got very angry and summoned his officers looking for the traitor. He was then told by one of his officers that Elisha the prophet was the one revealing his secrets to the king of Israel. This made the king of Aram even angrier. He sent out a great army of horses and chariots by night and surrounded the city where Elisha and his disciple were staying. When Gehazi woke up early the next morning, he saw that the city had been surrounded by a great army of Arameans; he ran to Elisha and asked "Alas, Master! What shall we do?" But Elisha replied, "Do not be afraid, for there are more with us than there are with them." Can you imagine what was going through Gehazi's mind? "I have always suspected that there might be something wrong with this man. Now I know he is a lunatic. He must be very crazy. There are over half a million soldiers out there, and only the two of us here and he is telling me not to worry. What in the world have I gotten my self into?" Elisha could read his fears. Elisha prayed, "O Lord, please open his eyes that he may see." "So the Lord opened the eyes of the servant, and he saw that the mountain was full of horses and chariots of fire around Elisha." God opened Gehazi's eyes to see the army of angels with horses and chariots of fire protecting him and Elisha. Elisha believed God for His promise of protection. He had the conviction of things not seen! He had faith in God.

We as Christians are gifted by God with this awesome gift of faith. We must learn to "walk by faith and not by sight" (2 Corinthians 5:7). To understand how to live by faith, we have to learn to start seeing things from the Divine viewpoint and not the human view point. The human viewpoint looks at life through the limitations of human wisdom, strength and resources, but the Divine view point looks at life through God's promises to work in us with His unlimited ability. Believe me, when the storms of life hit, you better be seeing things from the Divine point of view.

Faith in God can not exist without a loving obedience to God. Faith prompts us Christians to follow Christ's example and obey His commands. Obedience involves commitment of every aspect of our life to Him. We all know the story of Abraham in Genesis. God promised to make a great nation of him and his seed. This promise was made to Abraham when he was seventy-five years old, and Sarah his wife was sixty-five years old. God waited twenty five years to bless them with a son - Isaac. Everything was good until Isaac grew to his late twenties. God told Abraham to sacrifice his only son Isaac as a burnt sacrifice to Him. Abraham in obedient faith actually set out with Isaac to a mountain which God directed him to go. Now check this out, obedient faith in action. When Abraham arrived at the mountain, he said to his servants "Stay here with the donkey, the boy and I will go over there, we will worship, and then we will come back to you." (Genesis 22:5). Pay attention to what Abraham said, "We will come back to you."

What an incredible faith in God. Abraham must have thought, "You know God promised to give me this child. Although it took him twenty-five years to give me Isaac, He still kept His promise. Also God promised to make a great nation of me through this child. Isaac needs to be alive and have children of his own for God's promise of a great nation to be fulfilled. So if God requires me to offer Isaac as a burnt sacrifice, God would have to raise him up from the dead immediately, or else He would be failing in His promise. And He never fails to keep His promises." Waaoo! Abraham was very confident in God's faithfulness, when he said to the servants "We will come back to you."

We may not understand how and why God acts sometimes, but we can count on Him to provide for us if we faithfully obey Him. God did put Abraham to the ultimate test of faith and found him trust worthy. God expects us to use this great gift of faith He has given to every believer. God has put in us enough faith to blast through every mountain that gets in our way; and He expects us to use it. You complain you don't have enough faith, but that isn't the problem. The problem is that you have never developed your faith. Faith is like muscles that need to be stretched to its limit of endurance in order to build more strength. All you weight lifters know that we have to increase stress in training for muscle to grow. So it is with faith, it has to be tested to the limit of its endurance for it to grow. It takes times to develop a strong enduring faith. You cannot run a marathon without training. So come over to God's gym with the rest of us and start working out, so that the next time the devil comes bursting through your front door, you can stand up to him, and flex those big faith muscles.

CHAPTER NINE
The Helmet of Salvation

Ephesians 6:17a says "Take the helmet of Salvation." The helmet is needed to protect the head and the very vital organ of the brain. The brain is the main engine room of our mind. We absolutely need to protect the engine room of our minds from the deadly blows of Satan's relentless attacks against our salvation. Hence the need for the spiritual helmet of salvation. Satan uses a variety of attacks against us, and has planned schemes for our destruction. (Ephesians 6:11). 2 Corinthians 4:4 says, "In their case, the god of this world has blinded the minds of the unbelievers, to keep them from seeing the light of the gospel of the glory of Christ, who is the image of God." Satan is the god of this world because he is the evil of this world in person. Satan's major work is blinding people to the meaning of Jesus Christ and His gospel - eternal salvation.

Our firm faith in eternal salvation is one of the most important aspects of our defense. Satan knows that our eternal salvation is our eternal security. So he is always trying to knock off our helmets of eternal security in our salvation. We have to fight back by keeping our spiritual helmets of salvation firmly on our heads. If you don't have a spiritual helmet of salvation on your head, get one by accepting God's salvation today. 2 Corinthians 6:2b cautions us "See now is the acceptable time; see, now is the day of salvation." God's salvation is available today. Today provides the opportunity to accept God's salvation. Tomorrow may be too late.

What is salvation? Salvation is the process by which God redeems His creation, completed through the life, death and resurrection of His Son Jesus Christ. Salvation is a continuous process and it involves three steps - Regeneration, Sanctification and Glorification.

Regeneration

Regeneration is God's work in the believer at conversion to create a new person empowered by the Holy Spirit. Jesus tells us in John 3:3 - "Very truly, I tell you, no one can see the kingdom of God without being born from above." Here our Lord Jesus Christ was trying to explain the difference between the physical birth, (which Nicodemus asked about), and the new birth which Jesus said is very essential in order to see the Kingdom of God. The main point is clear - the physical birth is not enough, one must be born again spiritually to enter the kingdom of God. This contrast is emphasized in verses 5 and 6 - "Very truly, I tell you, no one can enter the kingdom of God without being born of water and Spirit. What is born of the flesh is flesh, and what is born of the Spirit is Spirit". Jesus described this new birth as a work of the Spirit.

Most Catholics especially those who are not part of the Catholic Charismatic Renewal are not familiar with the Baptism in the Holy Spirit. St. Paul in his letter to Titus said, "He saved us, not because of any works of righteousness that we have done, but according to his mercy, through the water of rebirth and renewal by the Holy Spirit. This spirit He poured out on us richly through Jesus Christ our savior." - (Titus 3:5 - 6). St. Paul was trying to explain to us that all three persons who make up the one being of God, share in the work of saving us. God is our savior, His love appeared in the person of Jesus, the son, and salvation includes the work of the Holy Spirit in renewing and purifying our lives. The Holy Spirit gives us hope of eternal life and encourages us to live morally pure lives. God's salvation is accomplished through the renewal by the Holy Spirit. This Spirit of the first creation (Genesis 1:2), is the same spirit of the new creation.

Baptism in the Holy Spirit could be explained as follows: In Baptism, God Himself came to live in us with all His gifts. Your Life is now immortal and your inheritance eternal. Confirmation brings more gifts. Isaiah 11:2 enumerates these gifts: - "The spirit of the Lord shall rest on him, the spirit of wisdom and understanding, the spirit of counsel and might, the Spirit of knowledge and the fear of the Lord." The exercise of all these gifts and graces presume our cooperation. I received the Baptism in the Holy Spirit as a young teenager in college. Before that experience, I was a vessel which God has filled with His gifts and charisms. In other words, I was like whole milk and Hershey's chocolate at Baptism and confirmation. But at my Baptism in the Holy Spirit, the hand of God through the Holy Spirit stirred this whole milk and Hershey's chocolate up to form a very unique blend of chocolate milk. Mmmm Yummy! At the Baptism in the Holy Spirit, all the gracious gifts we received at Baptism and Confirmation are fanned up into flame for the purpose, use and glory of God.

Personally, after my Baptism in the Holy Spirit, I noticed a definite change in all aspects of my life. I developed a very special and unique personal relationship with God. Going to mass meant a whole lot more to me. Praying my Rosary meant a whole lot more to me, as well. I developed an interest in reading my Bible, which I still do daily up to this day. I wanted more of God in my life. Weekly masses weren't enough any more for me. I started going to daily masses whenever possible. I joined a Bible study group because I wanted to learn more about my new found love Jesus and all His love letters to me in the Bible. I bought the Catechism of the Catholic Church and started studying more about my Catholic faith. I became so proud of who I am as a Catholic. I suddenly developed this boldness to tell perfect strangers about Jesus, my new found love. I would actually open my mouth and sing in church without being embarrassed about my not so angelic voice. The Blessed Mother Mary became a very special friend to me. The sacrament of reconciliation was not an obligation anymore for me, but it became an ongoing source of cleansing, healing and graces for me. When I fall - which I do very often - I run to God in the sacrament of reconciliation for His divine mercy, His graces and strength to turn away from sin and to pursue what is good and holy. Through regular confessions, the good Lord has opened my spiritual eyes, ears and mind to be more sensitive and sensible, and thus avoid the occasions of sin. This is an awesome gift for the believer.

After my Baptism in the Holy Spirit, the Holy Eucharist had a deeper new meaning to me. Lumen Gentum describes the Holy Eucharist as, "The Source and summit of Christian life." The words of the song in our Catholic Hymn Book - 'Gift of Finest Wheat' - say it all to me. "The mystery of your presence, Lord, no mortal tongue can tell: whom all the world can not contain comes in our hearts to dwell." When we receive the Holy Eucharist, Christ permits our mortal bodies to carry His body, blood, soul and divinity. Who can beat that? Even the angels in heaven don't have this wonderful and awesome privilege. I started spending time with Jesus in the Blessed Eucharist. This year, 2005 is the year of the Holy Eucharist. I encourage you to start spending some time with Jesus in the

Blessed Eucharist. It could be an hour a week or an hour a day. This is a method of prayer that will change your life forever. Bishop Fulton sheen, probably the most influential American Catholic bishop in history, made a vow at his ordination to spend an hour a day before the Blessed Eucharist. He was faithful to that commitment until the day he died. Our late pope, John Paul II spent some time everyday with Jesus in the Blessed Eucharist.

To any of my readers who have never received the Baptism in the Holy Spirit, please make an effort to call your diocese, and ask for a Catholic Charismatic Renewal group closest to you, and inquire on how to get the Baptism in the Holy Spirit. What did you think happened to our Blessed Mother Mary and the Apostles in the upper room on Pentecost day? They received the Baptism in the Holy Spirit. Pentecost was not for the Apostolic Church only; it is also for all of us today. "Thanks to the Charismatic Movement, many Christians have ... rediscovered Pentecost as a living and present reality in their daily life. I desire that the spirituality of Pentecost be spread in the Church, as a renewed thrust of prayer, holiness, communion and proclamation ..." Pope John Paul II, Pentecost 2004.

Sanctification

Sanctification is the process in Salvation by which God conforms the believer's life and character to the life and character of Jesus Christ through the Holy Spirit. It is an active process of being made holy by His gospel of grace. It involves a building process in the spiritual and ethical life of the believer. Sanctification leads to the participation in Christ's eternal inheritance - Glorification. Let's see what St. Paul told the elders of the church from Ephesus before he left for Jerusalem. He said, "And now I commend you to God and to the message of his grace, a message that is able to build you up and to give you the inheritance among all who are sanctified." (Acts 20: 32).

Sanctification is life in the Holy Spirit. The sanctified person bears the fruit of the Spirit, and crucifies his or her old sinful nature. Please note that this does not mean that the sanctified person is without sin. It does mean that we constantly fight against sin and yield ourselves to the Holy Spirit. Galatians 5: 22-25 tells us that, "The fruit of the spirit is love, joy, peace, patience, kindness, generosity, faithfulness, gentleness, and self-control. There is no law against such things. And those who belong to Christ Jesus have crucified the flesh with its passions and desires. If we live by the spirit, let us also be guided by the spirit." You see, the spirit of God is the Holy Spirit, not only is He holy, but one of His activities is to sanctify us, to make us holy. The Holy Spirit produces fruit in a Christian's life, but the Christian must be very cooperative. This cooperation from us is very important, or else the spirit cannot produce the fruit in us. Though the Holy Spirit leads us away from sin, He does not overwhelm us or force us to do God's will. Rather He offers us His gifts, power and guidance, and then expects us to follow Him. He gives us new life in Christ. The Christian life is a mystery. It's given completely by God, and He also gives us the Holy Spirit who alone can enable us to live up to the standards of God' love.

The life of a Christian is all done by the Holy Spirit of God within us. But still our active cooperation and passive yielding to the Holy Spirit of God calls us to obedience. Total obedience to God's will is the proof of repentance. The Spirit is not a possession we hold onto, but a "person" we love and obey. We must live the life to which we have been called to by God. We must trust God and His Spirit rather than ourselves.

Remember, a Christian must bear the fruit but only the Spirit can produce it.

Sanctification is the work of God which begins at regeneration and continues throughout life on earth. We are all God's work in progress. Sanctification is completed only in the life to come - and that is called Glorification.

Glorification

This is God's action in the lives of believers making them able to share the glory and the rewards of heaven. St. Paul in his letter to the Philippians said "I am confident of this, that the one who began a good work among you will bring it to completion by the day of Jesus Christ." (Philippians 1:6). God's faithfulness guarantees the completion of what He begins. He begins a good work of salvation in each believer at the time of conversion. He watches over its development and progression. The completion of the good work of grace will occur on the day Jesus returns in victory!

1 John 3:2 tells us this "Beloved, we are God's children now, what we will be has not yet been revealed. What we do know is that when he is revealed, we will be like him, for we will see him as he is." The prospect of glorification - of seeing Christ at His return is a purifying hope. This hope must be nurtured and cared for, especially in the face of persecution. To possess a steady hope that you will ultimately share in God's glory is a source of great joy. To see God is to become like Him at last. Since God is pure, purity is required to be like Him. The goal for us Christians is to become increasingly Christ-like, to be pure. Obeying the truth (all that Christ taught us) brings purity into our lives, a purity expressed in love for others. Obedience to God is the Christian's identifying mark.

STELLA IHUOMA NNANABU

CHAPTER TEN
THE SWORD OF THE SPIRIT

Ephesians 6:17b says "And the sword of the Spirit which is the word of God." The sword of the Spirit is the only offensive weapon we have in the armor of God. The other components of the armor are all defensive weapons. Let me take some time to describe the specific design of the Roman soldier's sword. The blade of the Roman soldier's sword was about twenty-four inches long and was sharpened on both sides. It was also sharply pointed on the end. The effectiveness of the design allowed the Roman soldier to thrust and cut with his sword from any position, so that he was never off balance. But the swords of the opposing soldiers of that time had large blades which were only sharp on one side. With this design, the opposing soldier had to position his arm at an angle and swing at the opponent in a chopping motion. This was disadvantageous to the opposing soldier because he was always cut off balance trying to reposition the arm for another swing.

Our sword is the word of God, the gospel message about Jesus Christ proclaimed by Christians. The word of God, the sword of the Spirit never leaves the believer off balance or out of position. The message about Jesus is found in both oral and written forms. St Paul confirmed this in Thessalonians 2:15 "So then, brothers and sisters stand firm and hold fast to the tradition that you were taught by us, either by word of mouth or by our letters." The written form is the Holy Scripture - the

Holy Bible. The Bible is the word of God, the sword of the Spirit. St. Paul in 2 Timothy 3:16-17 tells us that "All Scripture is inspired by God and is useful for teaching, for reproof, for correction, and for training in righteousness, so that everyone who belongs to God may be proficiently equipped for every good work." The word of God is called the Spirit's Sword because the Spirit uses the truth of the word of God to protect Christians against Satan. There is power in the word of God, and Satan knows this, and is terrified by it.

Jesus, Himself said "To you it has been given to know the secrets of the kingdom of heaven, but to them it has not been given." (Matthew 13:11). How would you have the "knowledge of the secrets of heaven"If you do not read the Bible - the word of God? You cannot use what you don't have. If you don't know anything about the word of God and all its promises, you cannot use it. Information is power. My dear fellow Catholics, it's about time we started reading and studying the word of God. If you don't own a Bible, please go to a Catholic bookstore and get one today. Get yourself a daily Bible reading guide too. There are so many resources out there to help and guide you in the study of the Bible. Join a Bible study group in your parish. Remember that the war is not against flesh and blood (not physical) but against the spiritual forces of evil in heavenly realms. This is a spiritual warfare. It takes fire to fight fire.

BIBLE = Basic Instruction Before Leaving Earth. Why is it that we rely on the manufacturer's manual to assemble our kids' toys, but we have refused to rely on God's manual to live the Christian life? God's word is alive and true. It's sharper than any two-edged sword, (Hebrews 4:12), and has the power to change lives and situations in our lives. Trust me, the more you read the word, meditate on it, live by it, the more your life will be changed by God's grace. We cannot live according to His word without being personally acquainted with His word.

My personal testimony is that for over twenty five years, I have been changed daily by spending time in the word, putting it in first place in my life. While I have changed, the process that changes me never has, - and that is, daily reading and meditation on the word of God. Proverbs 4:20 - 23 teaches us what the key to success in all areas of the Christian life is "My child, be attentive to my words, incline your ear to my sayings. Do not let them escape from your sight; keep them within your heart. For they are life to those who find them and healing to all their flesh. Keep your heart with all vigilance, for from it flows the springs of life." When you give your attention to the word of God, every other area in your life will be successful. Putting God's word in first place in your life is the answer to everything. This does not mean that you will not have problems. God's word shows us how to live victoriously, even in the face of problems.

With a daily focus on the word of God, you can fight the good fight of faith and even win when the storms of life come. (Remember the word of God is our spiritual sword.) Yes, the storms of life will surely come; Father Tom my parish priest always says "If it's not your turn today, it might be your turn tomorrow." Jesus told us a story about two men in Matthew's gospel. Both men heard the word but one man was foolish and the other was wise. The wise one acted on what he heard and the foolish one didn't. "Everyone who hears these words of mine and acts on them will be like a wise man who built his house on the rock. The rain fell, the floods came and the winds blew and beat on that house, but it did not fall, because it had been founded on rock." (Matthew 7: 24 - 5).

This is action time! You may know very well that you need

to spend time in the word, you may have heard it a thousand times, but hearing it isn't enough. Unless you take action now, today, not tomorrow, and set aside time for the word each day, you may not be prepared when the rains, the floods, the winds, (the storms of life) hit. No body in their right mind will try to build a house in a storm. So why are you waiting until you are desperate, to make time for the word of God? Please don't do that. Make the decision and start today. Then when the storms of life come against you, the word is the first thing out of your mouth. I know that we are all too busy, but the truth is that we don't have time not to study and meditate on the word of God. Don't let the devil talk you into being too busy for the word. I am a morning person, I wake up an hour earlier than I need to, to spend one hour studying and meditating on the word of God. Joshua 1:8 says "This book of law shall not depart out of your mouth; you shall meditate on it day and night, so that you may be careful to act in accordance with all that is written in it. For then you shall make your way prosperous and then you shall be successful." I call this God's three part formula for success:

1st = The book shall not depart out of your mouth

2nd = You will have to meditate on it daily

3rd = You will be careful to do everything in the book.

Then you will be prosperous and successful.

In regards to setting out time to study and meditate on the word, you know what time of the day works well for you. Pick a time of the day that suits you most. Have a date with the Lord in the word every day at this set time. My husband Jerry is an evening person so he does his Bible study and meditation in the evening after dinner. Even my three busy teenage kids find time to read their Bibles daily. Let me warn you because Satan knows how you tick. He will consistently send timestealers your way. So be on the alert. To be fore-warned is to be fore-armed! You see the time spent in studying and meditating on the word of God is your very life. It is where your victory lies and Satan knows this very well. Don't let your career, family, friends, extracurricular activities or anything else keep you away from a date with your beloved Lord and Savior every day. If you will give the word more time, it will give you more strength for the journey. And this is the supernatural strength you need to overcome when adversity strikes. Remember we are living in a fallen world, and these are the days of adversity. Look around, naturally speaking, things aren't getting any better in the world, things are in fact getting worst. Think about all the hurricanes, tornadoes, mudslides, fires, earthquakes and tsunamis of the recent months. These should make us aware of the times we are living in. These should not scare us, because 1 John 5:4 tells us that we Christians have conquered the world - "For whatever is born of God conquered the world. And this is the victory that conquered the world, our faith."

Even Jesus the master Himself used the sword of the Spirit when he was tempted by the devil in Matthew 4:1 - 11. He quoted Scripture verses to the devil that countered the temptation. So what are you waiting for, sharpen your sword and practice using it.

CHAPTER ELEVEN
PRAYER

Ephesians 6:18 says, "Pray in the Spirit at all times in every prayer and supplication. To that end keep alert and always persevere in supplication for all the saints." I think St. Paul had the modern day warfare in mind in the above verse. In modern day warfare, the enemy can be kept at a distance, and contained, by the use of heavy artillery. Prayer is our heavy artillery. We can keep Satan at bay so as to ward off his threatening danger by praying unceasingly. (1 Thessalonians 5:17).

An invasion by the Holy Spirit hit the Catholic Church over thirty-five years ago. The mystery of praying in tongues was unlocked in the Catholic Church. When we pray in tongues, we pray in the Spirit. When we pray in the Spirit, He guides us in God's will, and causes our prayer to be on target. St. Paul in Romans 8:26 - 27 explains this, "Likewise the Spirit helps us in our weakness, for we do not know how to pray as we ought, but that very spirit intercedes with sighs too deep for words. And God, who searches the heart, knows what is in the mind of the Spirit, because the Spirit intercedes for the saints according to the will of God."

Most times, we don't know what the perfect will of God is for us. This is when the Spirit comes to our aid. To pray in the Spirit is to be open to the Spirit's promptings and letting the Spirit pray in us, with us and for us according to the perfect will of God.

Sometimes in our prayers, we experience a profound sense of need, we may be without words for our prayers, and we may even realize that we cannot adequately express our love for God, our worship of Him, our sense of repentance, or even our requests to Him. This is when the Spirit steps in, to assist us in our prayers, praying within us and for us. I know for sure that when I pray in tongues, God answers my prayers.

The Holy Spirit is our advocate and comforter. When terrible things are happening in our lives, even things that we are not aware of, the Holy Spirit takes our prayers and starts to talk to Jesus who is at the right hand of the father in heaven. They communicate in a language we don't understand. But God knows the meaning of these tongues, and these prayers are in alignment with His great will and purpose. The intercession of the Spirit is on a communication level above the level of words. Within the Trinity, the communication is perfectly expressed and perfectly understood above any level or type of communication known to man. Thus when we pray in tongues, our prayers are translated into the high and noble level of God Himself.

Those who have never exercised this gift of the Holy Spirit should consider asking the Lord for this unique gift. This gift is there for the asking. Be open to the Spirit, be open to the gift of tongues and be willing to receive it. Again you can call your diocese for a Catholic Charismatic Renewal group closest to you. The group will provide you with instructions on the gift and even help you learn how to pray for it.

Intercession

Intercession is a prayer presenting the needs of others to God. This includes the needs of the Church and the world. This ministry can be done by any Christian who is willing to learn how and also willing to devote time to it. It can result in changed lives, changed church, and a changed world.

In 1 Timothy 2:1 - 4, St. Paul says, "First of all, then, I urge that supplications, prayers, intercessions, and thanksgivings be made for everyone, for kings, and all who are in high positions, so that we may lead a quiet and peaceable life in all godliness and dignity. This is right and is acceptable in the sight of God our savior, who desires everyone to be saved and to come to the knowledge of the truth." There is power in intercessory prayers. People in authority making important decisions especially, need our intercessory prayers, even though we may not know them personally and they may not be Christians.

Throughout the Old Testament, we find many examples of intercessory prayer for the nation of Israel, asking God for forgiveness, mercy, and restoration of the nation. In Esther 4:15 - 16, Esther prayed and fasted in preparation to go to the King. She needed dedicated prayer as she prepared to risk her life for her people. In Ezra 9:6 - 15, Ezra mourned over the sins of his people. His prayer bears the mark of deep repentance. Repentance is the appropriate way to deal with sin and guilt. It is the path to salvation. Sin starts a chain of consequences in the life of an individual, and then of a nation. It causes us to lose our standing and confidence with God. Ezra recognized that God is a righteous God who exposes His wrath against sin.

Nehemiah (in Nehemiah 1:5 - 11), like Ezra identified himself with sinful Israel and confessed Israel's sin to God. Nehemiah went a step beyond Ezra. He claimed the promises of the Holy Scripture, and asked for success as he initiated a plan to heal Israel. Confession of a nation's sin is an appropriate prayer before one undertakes a challenging project for God and His people. Nehemiah addressed his prayer to God in a way that expressed faith in the one unique God. The love of God, and the faithfulness of God are related attributes. The love of God for His people leads Him to exercise His faithfulness to His convent promises. These attributes make it possible for His people to pray to Him with trust that He will be faithful to answer in love.

So what is God saying to us? "If my people who are called by my name humble themselves, pray, seek my face, and turn from their wicked ways, then I will hear from heaven and will forgive their sin and heal their Land." (2 Chronicles 7:14). God is telling us to commit ourselves more to a righteous life and also pray for our nation. If we will do this, He promises to hear our prayers and restore our nation. We see a lot of moral breakdown and turning away from God in our nation today. The acceptance of abortion, the promotion of same sex marriage, embryonic stem cell research, human cloning, euthanasia; the sex abuse scandal in the church and the complete breakdown of sexual morality are all examples of our sins today. We need dedicated intercessors and prayer warriors like Ester, Ezra, and Nehemiah to intercede for our nation, the church, and our world.

We also need to intercede for our family and friends. But we have to find out what God's priority is for our family and friends. Jesus made this clear in Matthew 6:33, "But strive first for the kingdom of God and his righteousness, and all these things will be given to you as well." This is not an easy thing to do when we have a long list of material needs to pray for. We have to learn to pray for what God wants most and first. Don't misunderstand me, God wants us to pray for our human needs, but He wants to take care of the main thing first. As my pastor Father Tom would always say, "Let's keep the main thing, the main thing."

God is an all knowing God; His thoughts are not our thoughts and His ways not our ways. (Isaiah 55:8). All we have to do is just trust. "Trust in the Lord with all your heart, and do not rely on your own insight. In all your ways acknowledge him, and he will make straight your paths." (Proverbs 3:5 - 6). God's plan for us is much better than our plan for ourselves. He wants everybody in His Kingdom. God has a plan for each and every one of us. He said this in Jeremiah 29:11 - 12: "For surely I know the plans I have for you says the Lord, plans for your welfare and not for harm, to give you a future with hope. Then when you call upon me and come and pray to me, I will hear you." So let's learn to change the focus of our prayer for our family and friends. Let us pray according to the heart and spirit of God. Let us pray for the main thing first.

How about interceding for our neighborhoods? We are all aware of the local businesses in our neighborhoods that need lots of prayer - the abortion clinics, pornographic theaters, topless bars - the list goes on. Drive around your neighborhood very often, and pray for the conversion of the owners of such businesses and also for the people who patronize them. Sinful activities will die once hearts are converted to the Lord. Pray a lot for the forgiveness of sins and for the conversion of souls. Drive around the hospitals, nursing homes, prisons, juvenile detention centers, schools (grade schools, middle schools and high schools), colleges and high crime areas in your neighborhoods and pray for healing, for forgiveness of sins and conversion of souls. Remember, prayer is our heavy artillery, and we are trying to keep Satan at a distance by all our prayers.

Do we need to intercede for our enemies? Jesus says, "But I say to you, love your enemies and pray for those who persecute you." (Matthew 5:44). Are you praying for the people of Iraq and Afghanistan? Remember that they are created in God's image and likeness too. Jesus died for all mankind. Yes, he died for them too.

As you can see, there is a very great need for us, Christians to intercede for our nation, our church, our world, our enemies, family and friends. We need to reclaim our nation, our world, our neighborhoods, our families and our friends for the Lord who wants all to come to Him and not perish. God will surely hear our prayers and restore us. Amen!

I have a personal testimony on the power of intercessory prayer. I have a friend and a sister in Christ whose name is Joann Milich. Joann, we call her Jo, is a great intercessor and a very strong prayer warrior. She has a list of friends who she writes to every month and she calls us her pen pals. Just before Christmas 2004, Jo was led by the Spirit to start a twenty-one day "Daniel fast" for all her pen pals and all the people on her intercessory board. Not knowing the "why", Jo obeyed the Holy Spirit and started the fasting in December 2004. If you have ever fasted before, you will know that the holiday season is one of the toughest times to fast. Jo did it anyway.

After twenty-one days, she didn't hear from the Lord, so she decided to continue fasting for a total of forty days. She ended the fast on Friday January 21, 2005. In her January letter to all of us her pen pals, she made mention of her being led to fast for all of us. In her letter she said, "I am expecting great things, and I'm breaking strongholds in my life too!" She was not aware of my illness. When I got her January letter, I called her and we met for a glorious thirty minutes. She cried as I told her about my illness and hospitalization. You see the power of intercession in action. We prayed and praised God for His gift of inner peace in the face of adversity, His gift of spiritual stamina and courage in the face of intense and frightening circumstance, His gift of unshakeable hope and power in the face of a difficult and unpleasant situation. I thanked Jo for her obedience to the Holy Spirit.

Is God calling you to a deeper life of prayer as an intercessor and a prayer warrior? If your answer is yes, take a step in faith and say to the Lord as Isaiah did "Here I am, send me!" (Isaiah 6:8). God will anoint that step. Remember what happened with the Israelites in the book of Joshua. The waters of the Jordan River only parted when the priests stepped into the river. They took a step of faith in the face of an impossible task with the expectation that God's word will surely be accomplished (Joshua 3:13).

Don't come up with excuses for the Lord like Moses did when he was called, "I don't know your name," (Exodus 3:13). "What if the Israelites don't believe that you have sent me?" "I am not eloquent." (Exodus 4:10). Or like Jonah who tried to run away from God when he was called. Do not worry about your qualifications, your age, your nationality, because God equips whom He calls.

Think about our Blessed Mother Mary when she was called. She wasn't even a college graduate. She was not even the daughter of a rich king. Thinking about it myself, you know what I would have said to angel Gabriel if he had come to me with that news, "Has God lost His mind, is He crazy, He wants me to do what?" But Mother Mary said "Yes." Have you ever wondered what could have happened to humanity (you and I) if Mother Mary had not said "Yes". Scary to think about! I have always thought that God has a very high sense of humor. All through history; He always chooses the simple to confound the wise. Joseph in Genesis was just a slave boy. How about a second look at the qualifications of the twelve apostles of Jesus. Amazing, isn't it?

"Consider your own call, brothers and sisters: not many of you were wise by human standards, not many were powerful, not many were of noble birth. But God chose what is foolish in the world to shame the wise, God chose what is weak in the world to shame the strong; God chose what is low and despised in the world, things that are not, to reduce to nothing things that are, so that no one might boast in the presence of God." (1Corinthians 1:26 - 29). Surprising, isn't it? God works through people without worldly qualifications. No one can boast of attaining or deserving a position with God. Still God takes us into His service, and works through us to amaze those who claim proper credentials for success.

God has chosen each one of us to do something only we can do, and he will provide the grace, the strength, the ability and the means to accomplish what He asks of us. No one can replace you in the kingdom of God. Oh! Yes, you are that important in the eyes of God! We must be ready when God calls us to unusual tasks. This might mean coming out of our comfort zone, and going across many cultural barriers, and being misunderstood by many. But remember that no one can do your job in God's kingdom. No one can give your witness. We have to be ready when God calls to say, "Here I am Lord, send me!" You might be the only scripture some people out there might get to read before they die. THINK ABOUT THAT!!!

TO CONTACT THE AUTHOR WRITE TO:
Starlight Ministries

At WWW. Stellannanabu.Com

Please include your testimony or help received from this book when you write. Your prayer requests are welcome.